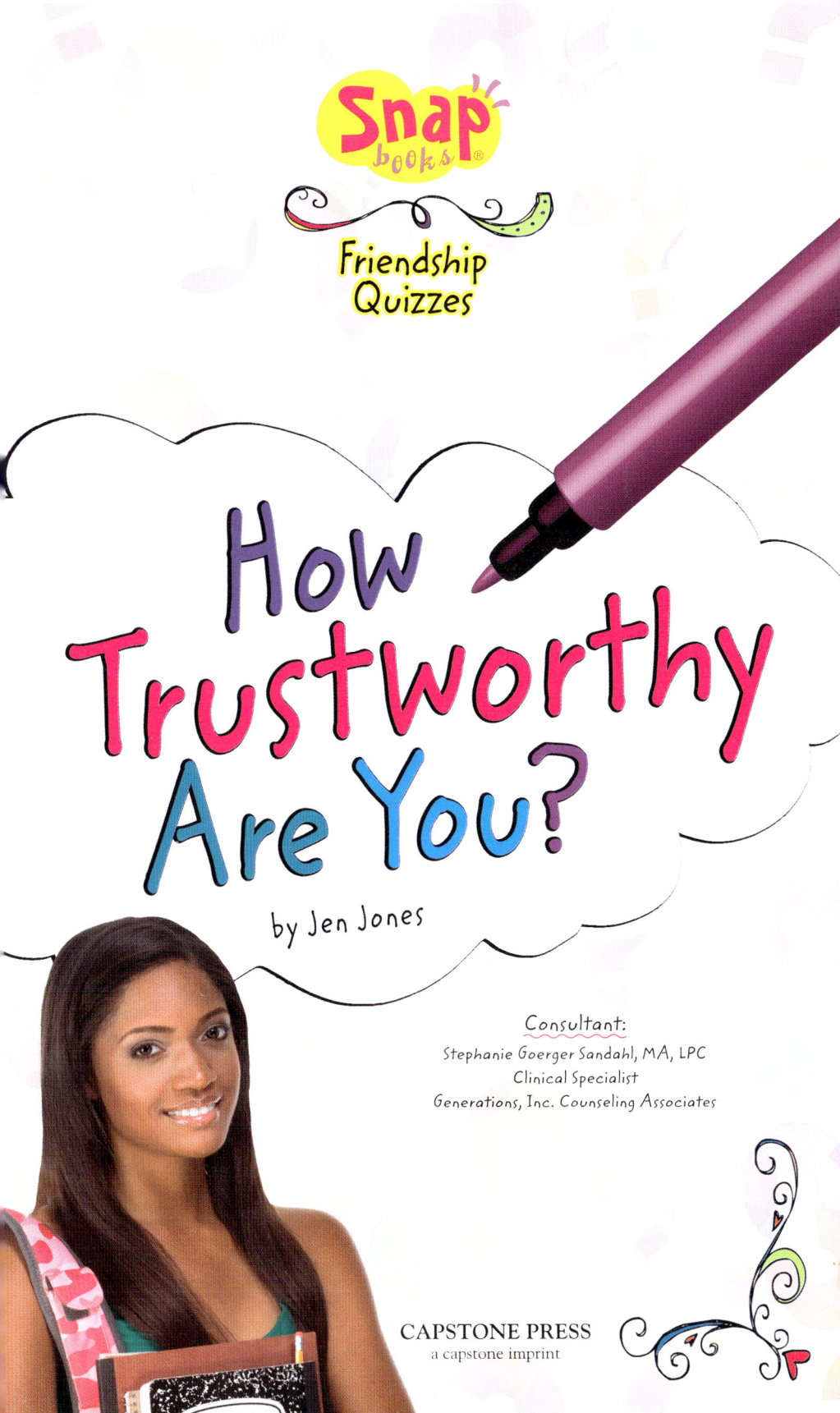

Snap books
Friendship Quizzes

How Trustworthy Are You?

by Jen Jones

Consultant:
Stephanie Goerger Sandahl, MA, LPC
Clinical Specialist
Generations, Inc. Counseling Associates

CAPSTONE PRESS
a capstone imprint

Snap Books are published by Capstone Press,
151 Good Counsel Drive, P.O. Box 669, Mankato, Minnesota 56002.
www.capstonepub.com

Copyright © 2012 by Capstone Press, a Capstone imprint.
All rights reserved. No part of this publication may be reproduced in whole or in part, or stored in a retrieval system, or transmitted in any form or by any means, electronic, mechanical, photocopying, recording, or otherwise, without written permission of the publisher.
For information regarding permission, write to Capstone Press,
151 Good Counsel Drive, P.O. Box 669, Dept. R, Mankato, Minnesota 56002.

 Books published by Capstone Press are manufactured with paper containing at least 10 percent post-consumer waste.

Library of Congress Cataloging-in-Publication Data
Jones, Jen.
  How trustworthy are you? / by Jen Jones.
    p. cm. — (Snap books: friendship quizzes)
  Includes bibliographical references and index.
  ISBN 978-1-4296-6539-1 (library binding)
  1. Trust. 2. Friendship. I. Title. II. Series.

BF575.T7.J66 2012
177'.62—dc22   2010044635

Editor: Brenda Haugen
Designer: Veronica Correia
Media Researcher: Marcie Spence
Production Specialist: Laura Manthe

Photo Credits:
Capstone Studio: Karon Dubke, cover, 4, 6, 10, 11, 14 (left), 16, 18, 20, 22, 23, 24, 27; Shutterstock: Alexey Lysenko, 14 (right), Alice (design element), Ayelet Keshet (design element), azzzya (design element), blue67design (design element), Booka, 9 (bottom), Edyta Pawlowska, 26, Elise Gravel (design element), Erick S., 9 (top), IKO, 8, Maaike Boot (design element), OLJ Studio, 1, oxygen64, 7 (background), Piotr Marcinski, 7 (front), Primusoid (design element), Sekulovski Ivo, 13, Todd Castor, 28, Tom&Kwikki (design element), UltraViolet (design element), zsooofija (design element)

Printed in the United States of America in Melrose Park, Illinois.
032011   006112LKF11

Table of Contents

Introduction 4
Quiz 6
Results 18
Glossary 30
Read More 31
Internet Sites 31
Index 32

Introduction

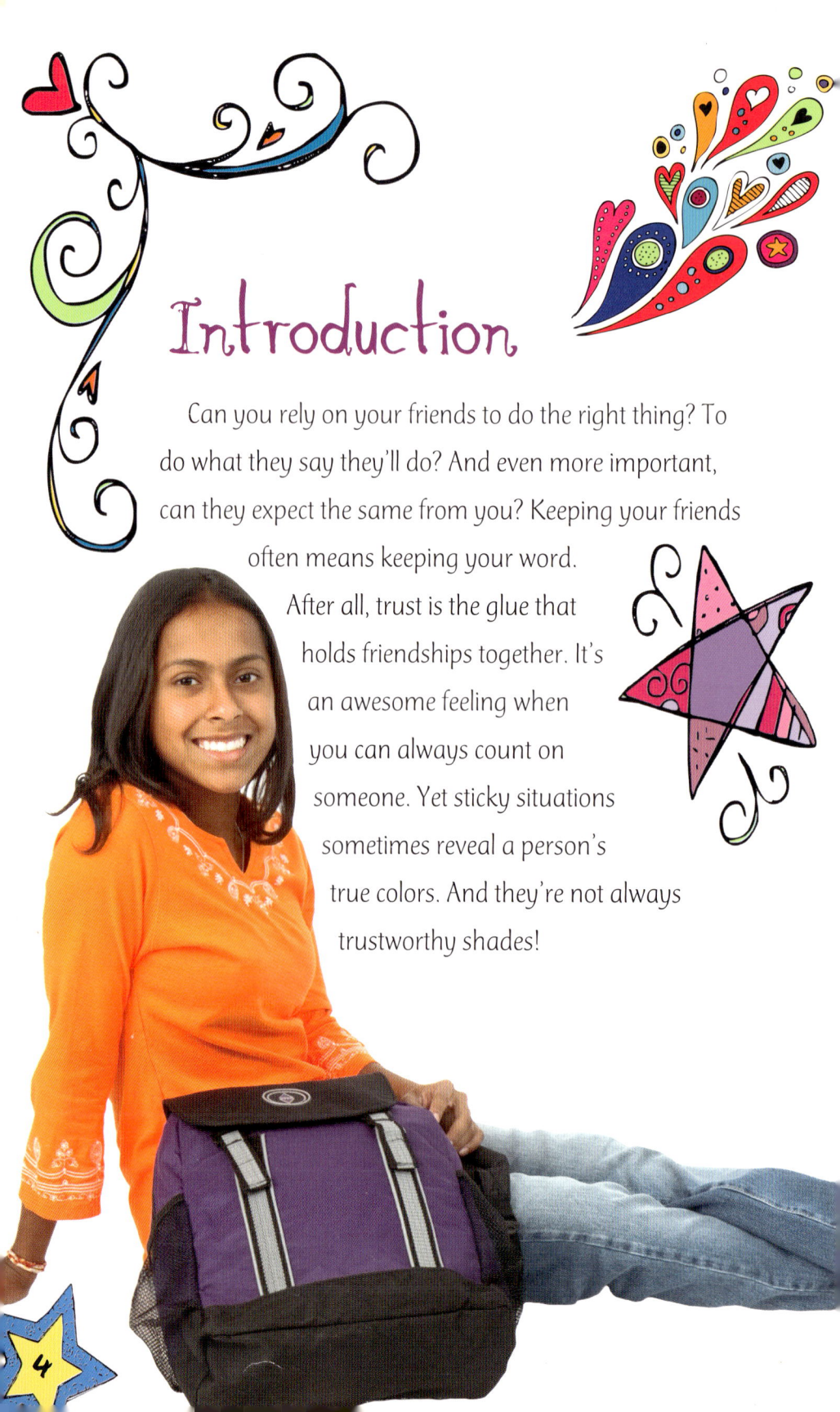

Can you rely on your friends to do the right thing? To do what they say they'll do? And even more important, can they expect the same from you? Keeping your friends often means keeping your word. After all, trust is the glue that holds friendships together. It's an awesome feeling when you can always count on someone. Yet sticky situations sometimes reveal a person's true colors. And they're not always trustworthy shades!

Though you can't control other people, you can work on building your own trust factor. The first step is to take this fun quiz to see where you rank on the trust-o-meter. Can your friends really depend on you? Depends on how you do!

Even though this is nothing like taking a test at school (it's way cooler!), there are a few things you'll need before you get started. And don't worry—no #2 pencils required.

• Grab a sheet of notebook paper to write your answers down. You'll also need a pen or pencil. Number the sheet from 1 to 16, and you're ready to rock!

• Tell the truth. No one will see your answers but you.

AND PLEASE, DO NOT WRITE IN THIS BOOK!!!

OK ... ready, set, grow!

QUIZ

1- Your friend tells you a juicy secret. You promise not to tell anyone. This means:

a) That I really won't tell anyone. But if I do spill the beans, I'll make them pinky-swear never to tell a soul.

b) I'll try, but I've been known to blab here and there.

c) My lips are sealed, Super Glue-style.

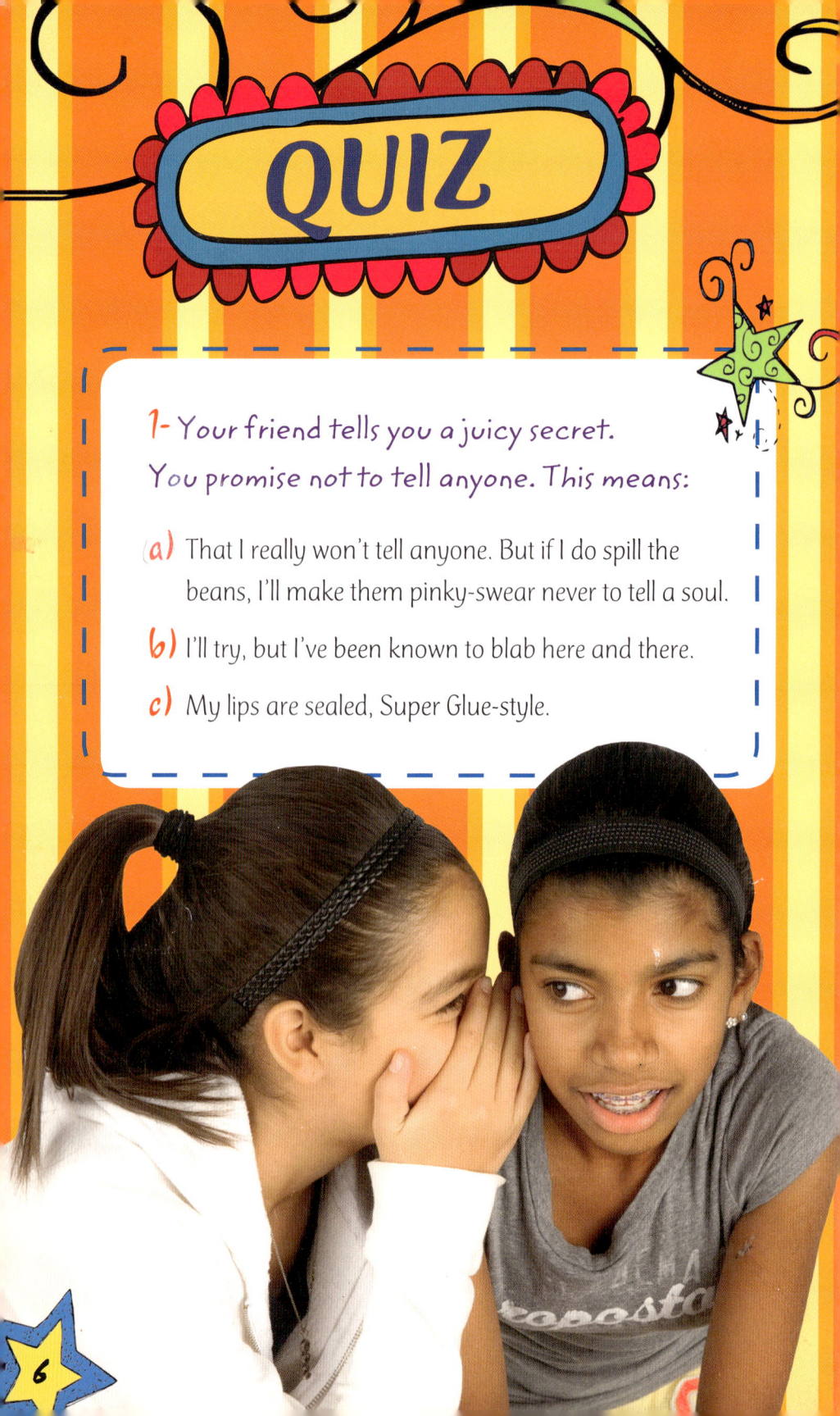

2- You need money to go to the movies, but you already spent your allowance. You discover Mom sometimes hides cash in the cookie jar. What do you do?

a) Take only the exact amount you need, and leave a note promising to pay it back.

b) Leave the money alone, and stay home from the movie.

c) Sneak a few bucks. She'll probably never notice.

3- Whoops! Your sister accidentally leaves her Facebook account open. What happens next?

a) It's super-tempting to sneak a peek, but you close it out for her without looking.

b) You post a message revealing her secret crush. She'll thank you when the guy finally finds out!

c) You take a quick scroll through her messages folder and tease her about the posts later.

4- When you get mad at one of your friends, you usually:

a) Talk to everyone about it but her.

b) Tell her you're mad—and why you're mad! With **tact**, of course.

c) Hold it in for a while. But at some point, you fess up to what's bugging you.

5- Every Tuesday you help your biology teacher clean the fish tanks after school. But when a friend says she has two free tickets for the newest vampire flick, it's pretty tempting. You:

a) Ask your friend to help you out in the biology lab. You'll offer to pay for tickets to see the movie another time.

b) Leave the teacher a note that you'll clean the tank first thing in the morning. You're sure he'll understand.

c) Feel a little guilty, but blow off the fishies. You're off to check out the vampires!

6- It's your lucky day: you find a $20 bill on the floor at a restaurant! You:

a) Look around to see who might have dropped it. If no one seems to be looking for the money, you can pocket it.

b) Turn it in to the restaurant manager. After all, you'd want someone to do that if it was your money.

c) Snatch it up immediately! Finders keepers.

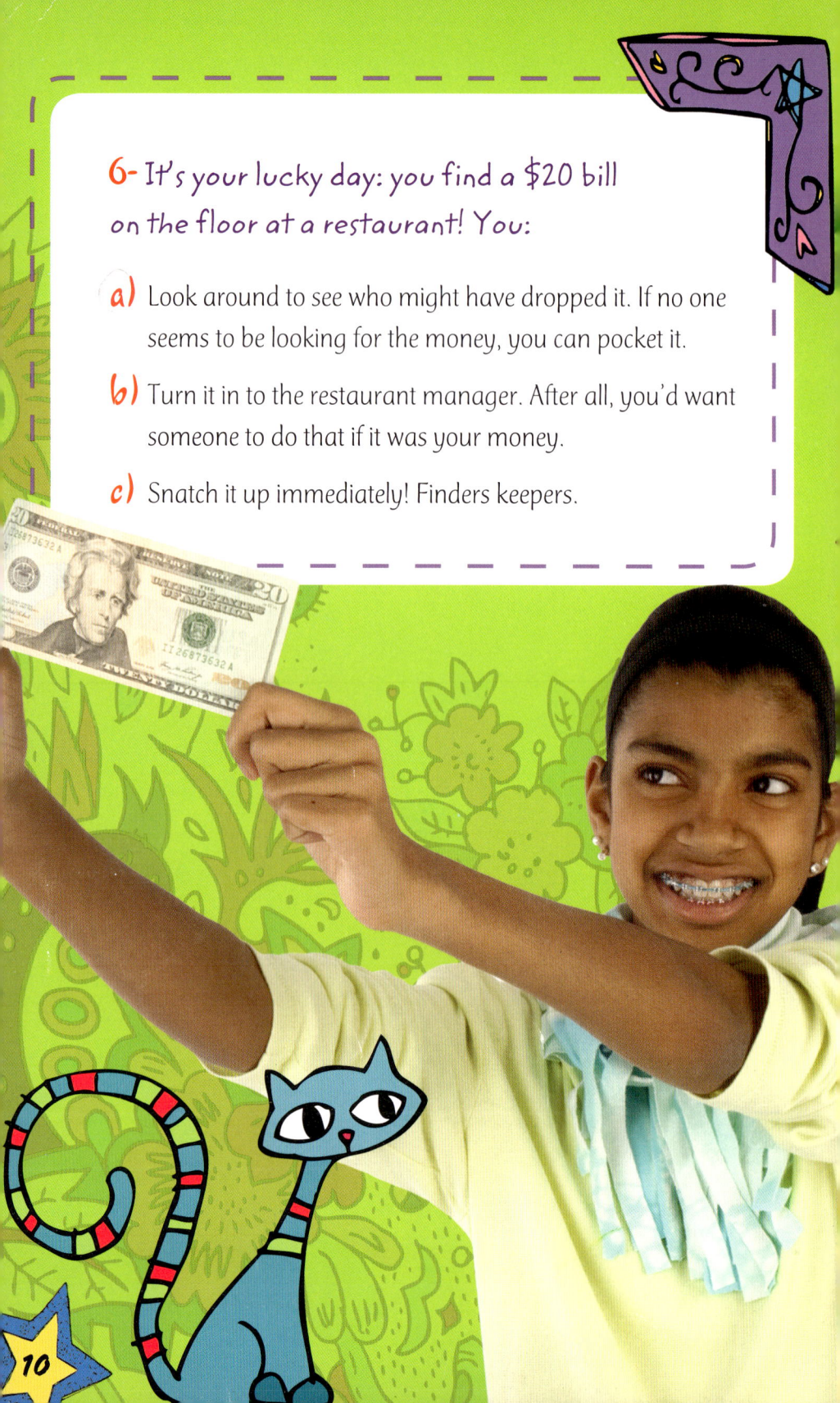

7- Rate your flake factor: How often do you break plans?

a) Rarely if ever, unless an emergency pops up.
b) All the time! My mood changes a lot, and I can't be tied down to plans.
c) Sometimes, especially when a can't-miss opportunity comes along.

8- What's one thing you wish you could change about yourself?

a) Not being such a gossip.
b) Always being late.
c) Trusting others too much.

9- You're totally stuck for a song to perform in the school talent show. You overhear a classmate rehearsing one that would be perfect for your voice. What do you do?

a) Talk to the teacher to see if it's OK if two people do the same song.

b) See if your classmate will help you brainstorm another great tune.

c) Try to talk her out of performing the song.

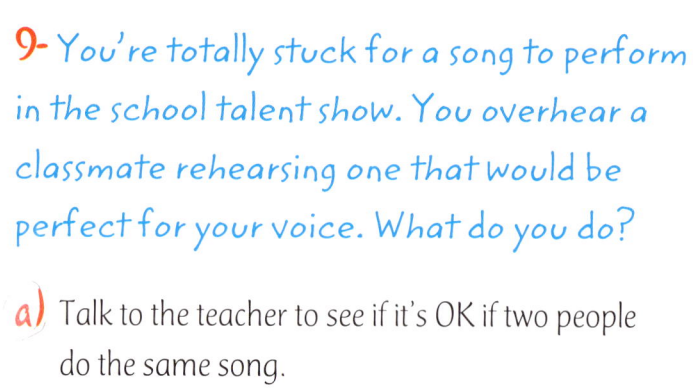

10- It's Tuesday, which means softball practice after school at 3:30. At 3:31, where are you?

a) On your way home to chill and watch some TV. You're just not in the mood to practice today!

b) In uniform, on the field, and ready to go.

c) Still in the locker room rushing to get ready. Somehow you always seem to be running five or 10 minutes behind.

11- One of your friends isn't the most reliable girl on the planet. When she's 30 minutes late to a smoothie date, your reaction is:

a) I better call to make sure she's OK.

b) Smoothie-to-go, please!

c) Ten more minutes, and then I'm out of here.

12- Score! You and a friend win tickets to meet your favorite indie rock band. At the concert, he snags the last signed poster and CD, which you totally wanted. When he forgets them in your mom's car, you:

a) Promise you'll give them back soon … once you scan in the poster and burn a copy of the CD.

b) Call him right away to see when he'll pick them up.

c) Keep them, and keep quiet. He'll probably forget where he left them.

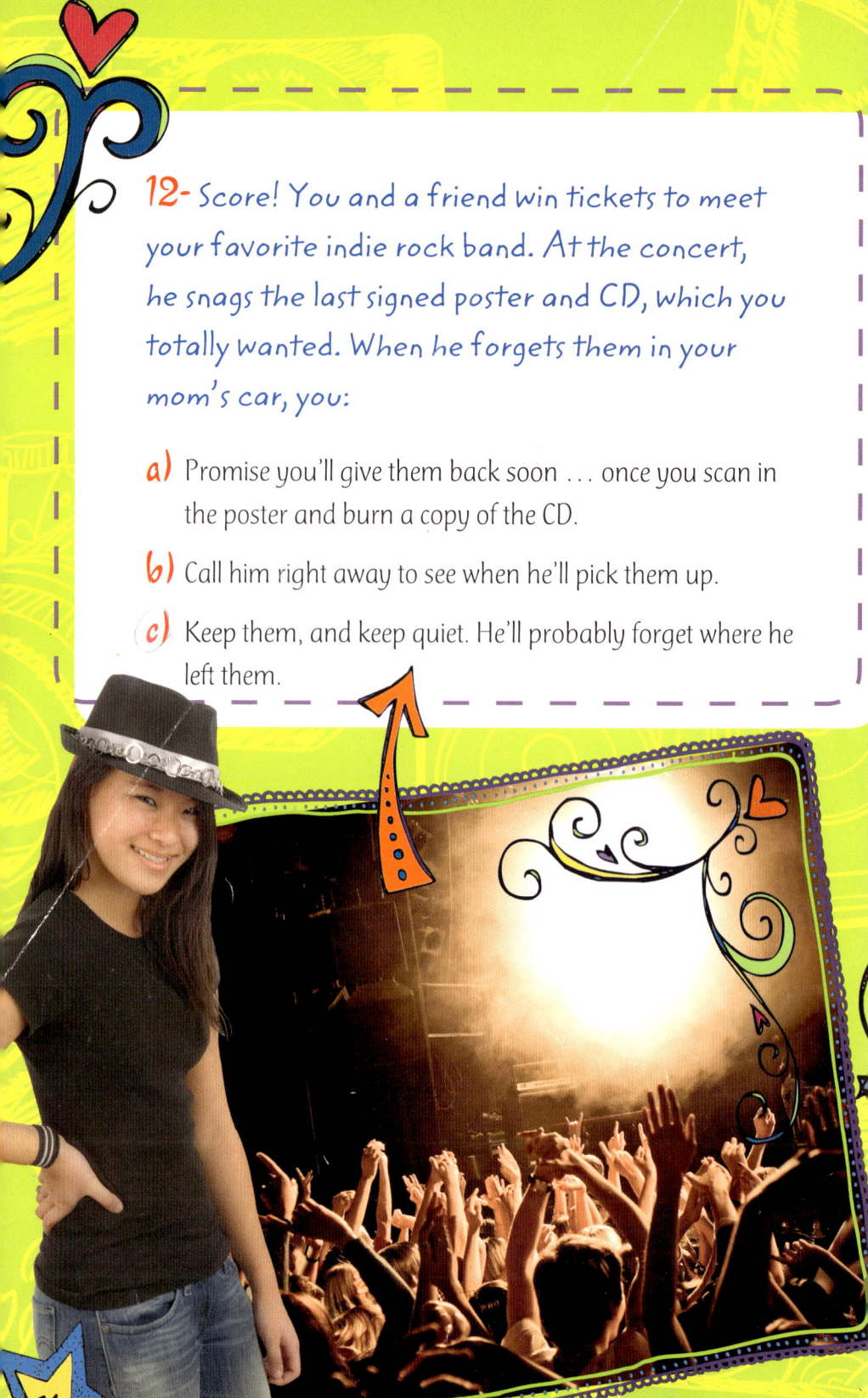

13- Your parents are going out for date night, which means you're allowed to have a friend come over! After your parents leave, another pal texts to see if she can join in the fun. You write back:

a) "Sorry, but I'm allowed to have only one friend over. Let's get together next time they go out."

b) "Hmm, well, do you think you could leave before my parents get home? I'll be in big trouble if I get caught."

c) "Only if you bring pizza and magazines!"

14- Your sister finally lets you borrow her favorite shirt. You get a tiny stain on it. What do you do?

a) Frantically count your allowance. Maybe you can buy her a new one, and she'll never know the difference!

b) Try to scrub out the stain and hope she won't notice.

c) Fess up right away and offer to pay for dry-cleaning the shirt.

15- When you take magazine quizzes, you:

a) Choose your answers honestly. After the quiz is complete, you check to see what they mean.

b) Tend to peek at the answers before you're done taking the quiz.

c) Try to pick the "right" answers to get the results you want!

16- The most important quality I look for in a new friend is:

a) A forgiving nature.

b) Reliability.

c) A sense of fun.

Don't turn the page yet!

It's time to tally your results. Check your answers below. Jot down the number of points you scored for each answer, and then add up your points.

1. a—2; b—3; c—1
2. a—2; b—1; c—3
3. a—1; b—3; c—2
4. a—3; b—1; c—2
5. a—1; b—2; c—3
6. a—2; b—1; c—3
7. a—1; b—3; c—2
8. a—3; b—2; c—1
9. a—2; b—1; c—3
10. a—3; b—1; c—2
11. a—1; b—3; c—2
12. a—2; b—1; c—3
13. a—1; b—2; c—3
14. a—2; b—3; c—1
15. a—1; b—3; c—2
16. a—3; b—1; c—2

Turn to page 18 if you scored 16 to 26 points.

Turn to page 22 if you scored 27 to 37 points.

Turn to page 26 if you scored 38 to 48 points.

RESULTS

16 to 26 points:

TRUSTY AS CAN BE

Your word is so golden that you're like a ray of sunshine for those around you!

The Full Scoop

Everyone needs a friend who can be counted on. And that person is you! When a friend is crying, you offer a shoulder. When your friend has broccoli in her teeth, you're there with the mirror. When your parents need a babysitter, they can depend on you. You try really hard to keep your word. And for that you get R-E-S-P-E-C-T.

Real-Life Rx: Tips You Can Use

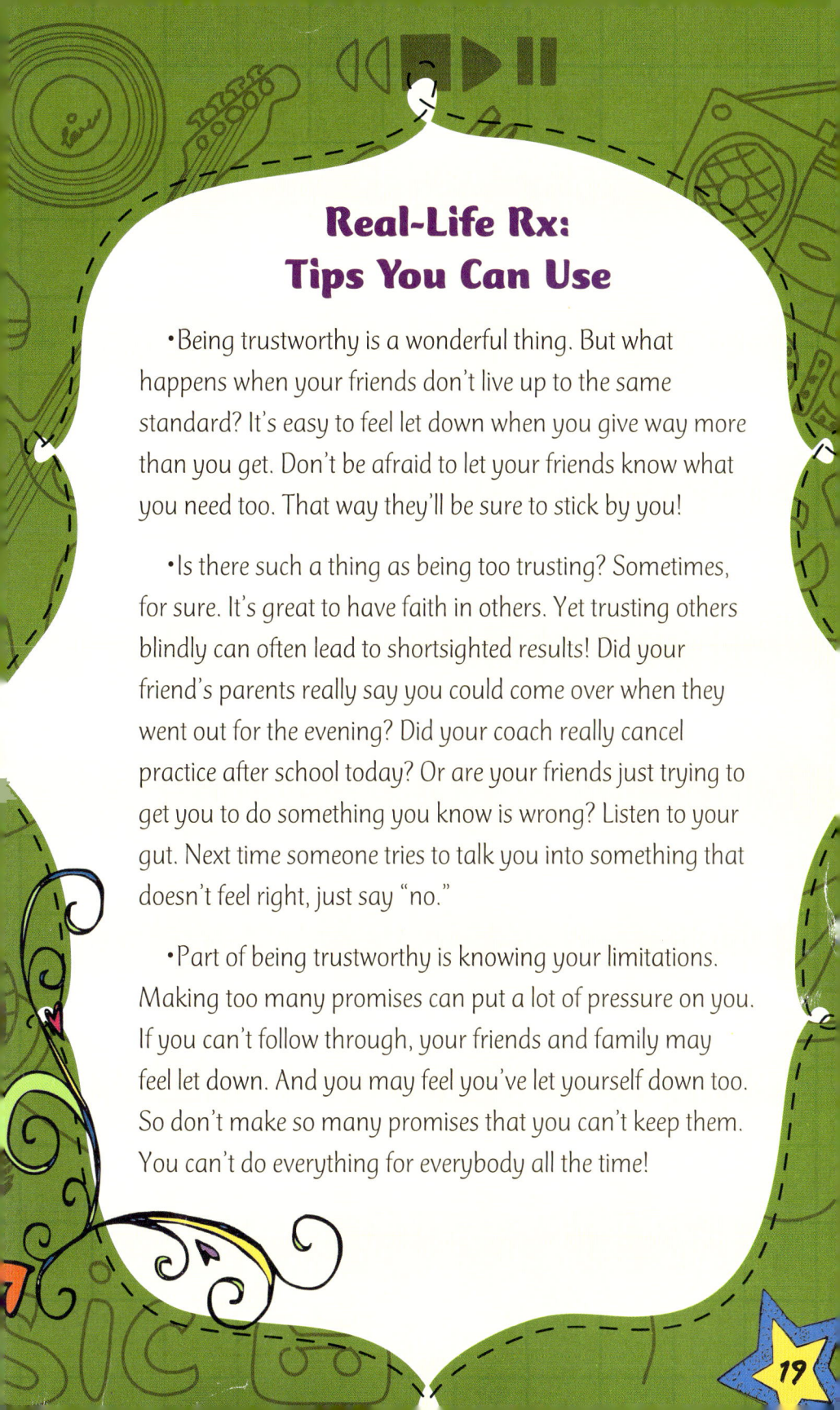

- Being trustworthy is a wonderful thing. But what happens when your friends don't live up to the same standard? It's easy to feel let down when you give way more than you get. Don't be afraid to let your friends know what you need too. That way they'll be sure to stick by you!

- Is there such a thing as being too trusting? Sometimes, for sure. It's great to have faith in others. Yet trusting others blindly can often lead to shortsighted results! Did your friend's parents really say you could come over when they went out for the evening? Did your coach really cancel practice after school today? Or are your friends just trying to get you to do something you know is wrong? Listen to your gut. Next time someone tries to talk you into something that doesn't feel right, just say "no."

- Part of being trustworthy is knowing your limitations. Making too many promises can put a lot of pressure on you. If you can't follow through, your friends and family may feel let down. And you may feel you've let yourself down too. So don't make so many promises that you can't keep them. You can't do everything for everybody all the time!

Your Imaginary Alter Ego:
Rocky Blue from Shake It Up

A true friend will never leave you in the dust—even when she's about to hit it big! Take Rocky (played by Zendaya Coleman) from Disney's "Shake It Up." Her BFF, Cece, blows her big dance audition. Yet Rocky refuses to go on without Cece by her side. She even cuffs their hands together to get the judges to notice Cece's star power! Pretty impressive for someone who could have stolen the spotlight and focused on her own fame.

What Would You Do?
Girls Talk Back

Get straight-up advice from girls who've been there, done that.

Did You Know?

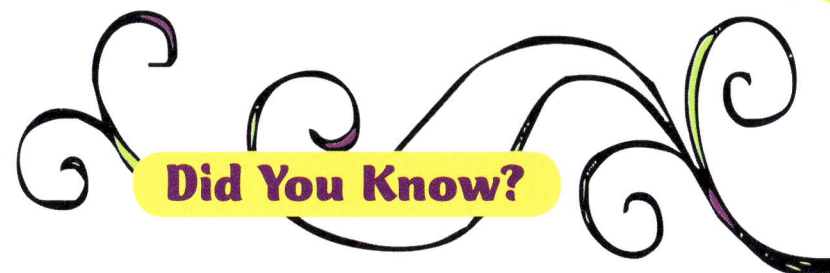

✶ Do you always trust in what others tell you? Those beliefs may have started when you were just a tiny tot. Studies show that many young kids will often believe what adults tell them, even if they can see it's not true.

Q: Every time I share something with my BFF, she makes it a competition. If I admire a cool backpack at the mall, she's sporting it the next day. If I get a "B" in science class, she brags about her "A"! It's starting to feel like we're competing all the time.

A: Newsflash—this behavior definitely isn't the mark of a forever friend! Good friends boost you up, instead of bringing you down. Maybe she's competitive by nature. Or maybe she admires you so much she wants to be just like you. But in order to keep the friendship flowing, it's time to have a talk about her behavior. Once she knows how it makes you feel, see if she keeps doing it. Then you'll know whether you can really trust her ... or not.

27 to 37 points:
SLIPPING A BIT

You don't push the trust limits too far. Yet you still tend to test the waters of trust. Over time, that can definitely have a ripple effect on your relationships.

The Full Scoop

Being trustworthy isn't always black and white. Sometimes situations fall into a gray area. In those cases, it's hard to know if you're doing the right thing. Sure, you don't openly double-cross your friends. But sometimes your actions do let them down. Maybe you're always late. Or maybe you break plans at the last minute. Put it this way. If trust was a scale of 1 to 10, you'd be sitting at about 6. So how can you ramp it up closer to 10? There are tons of ways. Be more honest. Keep your promises. Don't go behind others' backs to do or say things. Put these ideas in practice, and your trustworthiness can go from gray to a rainbow of colors!

Real-Life Rx: Tips You Can Use

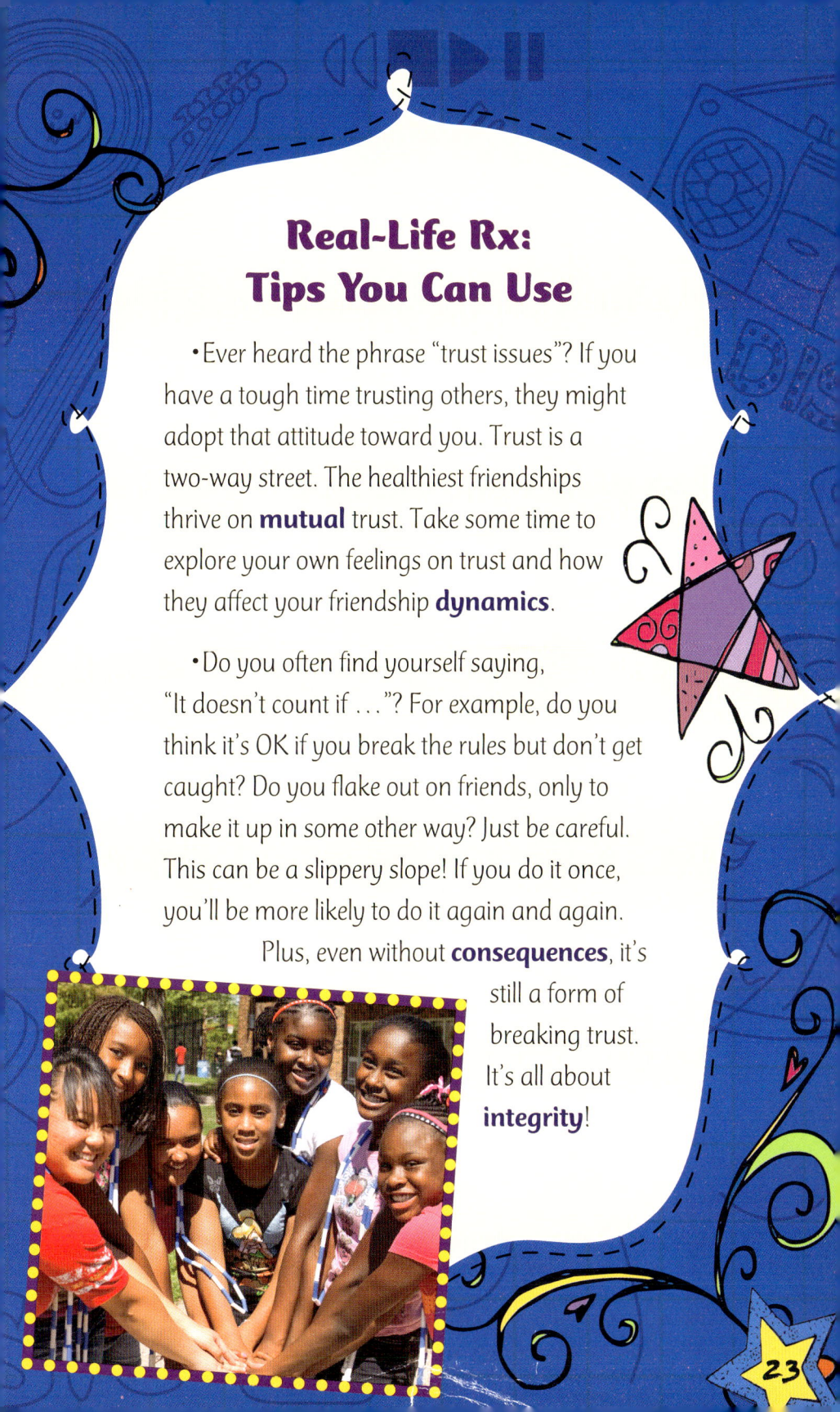

• Ever heard the phrase "trust issues"? If you have a tough time trusting others, they might adopt that attitude toward you. Trust is a two-way street. The healthiest friendships thrive on **mutual** trust. Take some time to explore your own feelings on trust and how they affect your friendship **dynamics**.

• Do you often find yourself saying, "It doesn't count if . . ."? For example, do you think it's OK if you break the rules but don't get caught? Do you flake out on friends, only to make it up in some other way? Just be careful. This can be a slippery slope! If you do it once, you'll be more likely to do it again and again. Plus, even without **consequences**, it's still a form of breaking trust. It's all about **integrity**!

Your Imaginary Alter Ego: Alex Russo from Wizards of Waverly Place

Wizards are complex creatures. Alex (played by Selena Gomez) is no exception! Sometimes sneaky and always making mischief, Alex often lies to her loved ones. It's hard to trust Alex. She's known for casting spells to make things go her way. Yet those same powers are often used to protect her brother, Justin, and best friend, Harper. This wizard-in-training definitely has a big heart underneath that sly surface! With Alex, what you see isn't always what you get.

What Would You Do? Girls Talk Back

Get straight-up advice from girls who've been there, done that.

Did You Know?

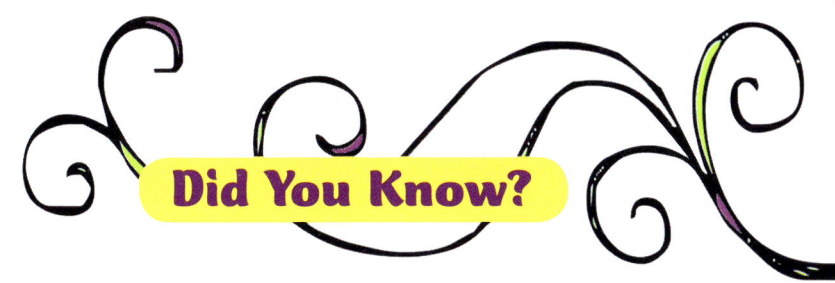

Wondering whom you can trust most? Maybe it's time to "face" the facts! Professors at Princeton University have discovered that people often decide whom to trust based on looks. People believe those with wide eyes and U-shaped mouths are most trustworthy. Lowest on the trust totem are those with eyebrows pointing down in the center and people who are always frowning.

Q: Here's my issue: I can't seem to keep a secret! How can I fix the problem before I get labeled as a total big-mouth?

A: You're not alone. Research shows that four out of 10 girls can't keep a secret. But like you, 66 percent of secret-spillers feel guilty after letting the info loose! The good news is it's never too late to become a trusted **confidant**. One tip would be to trust your friend right back and share a secret of your own. After all, you'll be less likely to spread her scoop around if yours is at risk too! Another approach is to be straight up. Say, "I know I've accidentally blabbed in the past, but I'm working on it. I hope you'll trust me in the future." Odds are you'll get a second chance. It's up to you to show your friends you deserved it!

38 to 48 points:

TIME FOR A RELIABILITY BOOST

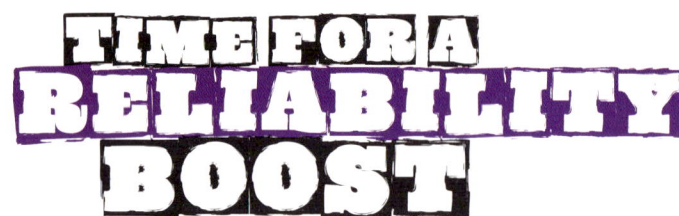

On the trust-meter, your tank is running a little low! Maybe it's time to refuel your friendships with a new attitude.

The Full Scoop

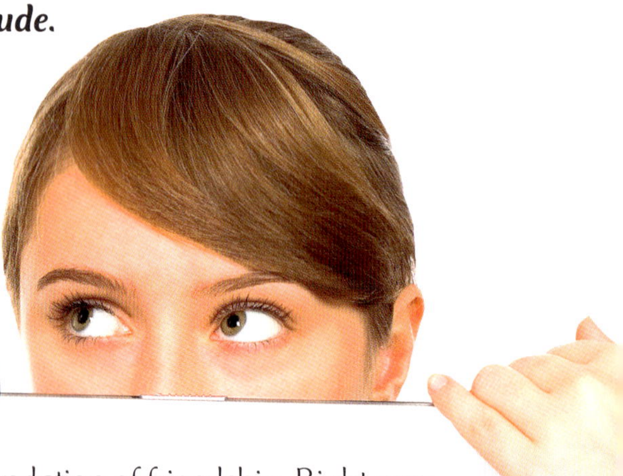

Trust is the foundation of friendship. Right now your friendships may be on rocky ground. Without trust, it's hard for friends to confide in you or turn to you in times of need. Think about it. Have you ever embarrassed a friend by telling a secret? Have you ever tattled just to get someone in trouble? Have you talked behind your friends' backs? These are lots of levels to losing trust. These are just a few of them. If you've been guilty of any of these things, some relationship repair might be in order.

Real-Life Rx: Tips You Can Use

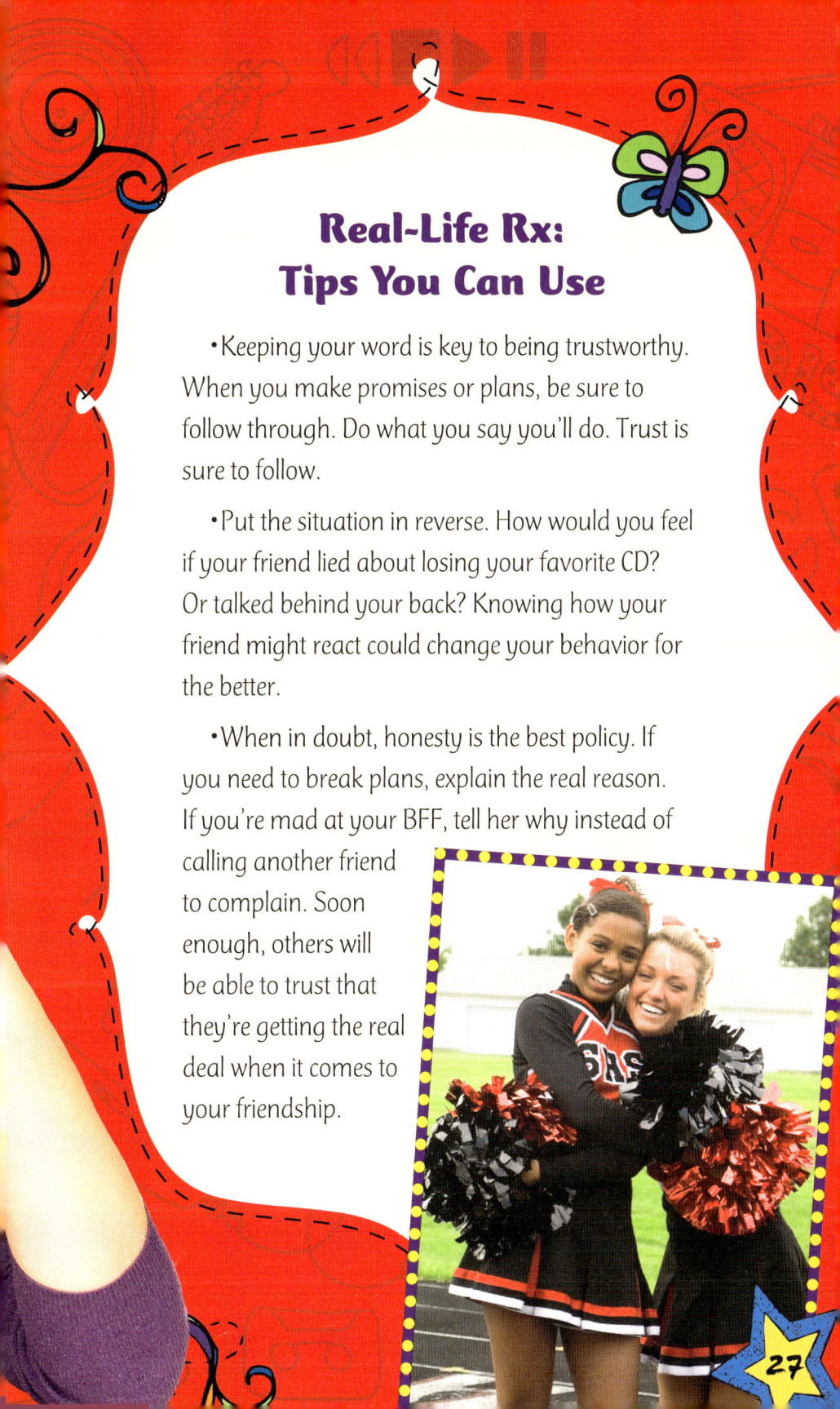

• Keeping your word is key to being trustworthy. When you make promises or plans, be sure to follow through. Do what you say you'll do. Trust is sure to follow.

• Put the situation in reverse. How would you feel if your friend lied about losing your favorite CD? Or talked behind your back? Knowing how your friend might react could change your behavior for the better.

• When in doubt, honesty is the best policy. If you need to break plans, explain the real reason. If you're mad at your BFF, tell her why instead of calling another friend to complain. Soon enough, others will be able to trust that they're getting the real deal when it comes to your friendship.

Your Imaginary Alter Ego:
Anna McMasters from Beacon Street Girls

Signs show you might have lots in common with Beacon Street's resident "Queen of Mean." From social **sabotage** to starting an IM gossip chain, Anna has pulled almost every trick in the untrustworthy book. And she usually ropes in her friend Joline, creating double the drama! If your relationships are starting to resemble hers, it might be time to turn the page and start a new chapter.

What Would You Do?
Girls Talk Back

Get straight-up advice from girls who've been there, done that.

Did You Know?

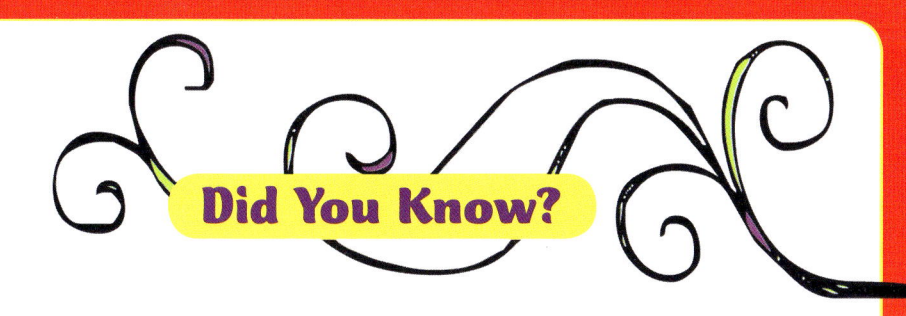

A 2010 **psychology** study on trust found that people fall into two categories. Some believe that a person is either born trustworthy or not. People who think this way have a harder time rebuilding trust once it has been broken. Others think that trust depends on the situation. These people may be more likely to give someone a second chance.

Q: I read my friend's journal, and she caught me in the act. How do I earn her trust back? Help!

A: The first step is to have patience. After all, trust can't be earned back overnight. And, in some cases, the reality is that it's never fully restored once broken. But if you're serious about showing her you deserve forgiveness, there are a few things you can do. Admit you messed up. See if she's willing to start fresh. If so, ask what you can do to start your new relationship off right. Promising not to share her journal secrets with anyone is a good start, as long as you mean it.

Glossary

confidant (KON-fuh-dawnt)— someone you can trust with secrets

consequence (KAHN-suh-kwens)— result of your actions

dynamic (dye-NAM-ik)— the changing atmosphere of a group

integrity (in-TEG-ruh-tee)— total honesty and sincerity

mutual (MYOO-choo-uhl)— shared

psychology (sye-KOH-luh-jee)— the study of the mind, the emotions, and human behavior

reliability (re-lye-uh-BIH-leh-tee)— state of trustworthiness and dependability

sabotage (SAB-uh-tahzh)— to damage, destroy, or interfere with on purpose

tact (TAKT)— a way of being honest without hurting someone's feelings

Read More

Brown, Lauren, Ed., **and from the Creators of Girls' Life Magazine.** *Ultimate Guide to Surviving Middle School.* New York: Scholastic, 2010.

Lynch, Amy. *A Smart Girl's Guide to Understanding Her Family: Feelings, Fighting & Figuring It Out.* Be Your Best. Middleton, Wis.: American Girl, 2009.

Reece, Gemma. *The Girls' Book of Friendship: How to Be the Best Friend Ever.* New York: Scholastic, 2010.

Internet Sites

FactHound offers a safe, fun way to find Internet sites related to this book. All of the sites on FactHound have been researched by our staff.

Here's all you do:

Visit *www.facthound.com*

Type in this code: 9781429665391

Check out projects, games and lots more at
www.capstonekids.com

Index

angry feelings, 8, 27

Beacon Street Girls (books), 28
blind trust, 19
Blue, Rocky (fictional character), 20

Cece (fictional character), 20
Coleman, Zendaya, 20
competition, 21
consequences, 23

Facebook, 8
forgiveness, 16, 25, 29
friendships, 4, 6, 8, 9, 13, 14, 15, 16, 18, 19, 20, 21, 22, 23, 25, 26, 27, 29

Gomez, Selena, 24
gut instincts, 19

honesty, 15, 16, 22, 24, 27

integrity, 23

limitations, 19, 22
looks, 25
lying. *See* honesty

McMasters, Anna (fictional character), 28
money, 7, 10
mutual trust, 23

Princeton University, 25
promises, 6, 11, 14, 19, 22, 27, 29

reliability, 9, 12, 13, 16, 18, 22, 27
Russo, Alex (fictional character), 24

secrets, 6, 25, 26, 29
Shake It Up (TV show), 20
stealing, 7, 14

Wizards of Waverly Place (TV show), 24